I
OF
MODERN NATURE

By

Richard Wheeler

Print ISBN 978-1-8384289-8-3

Published 2021 by
Llyfrau Cambria Books, Wales, United Kingdom.
*Cambria Books is a division of
Cambria Publishing.*
Discover our other books at: www.cambriabooks.co.uk

What they say

"From city boulevard to submerged forest, the streets of Paris to 'the nonchalance of pike' in shadows, Richard Wheeler's vivid and sharply observed poems draw the reader into a sensuous world of colour, sound and texture. These are carefully crafted and haunting pieces, inspired by the poet's love of music, art and nature, and reflecting on our own relationships with the world and those around us.
A stunning debut collection, and certainly one to treasure."

Kathy Miles, poet from West Wales, winner of the 2015 Bridport Prize. Her fourth full collection is *Bone House*.

*

"This is a confident and highly accomplished debut that comes from a place of deep lyrical reverence for the natural world and consummate understanding of the human condition. Richard creates keenly observed tableaux in a taut, muscular and personal concision that draws the reader ever inwards. He is a promising poet who delivers from a rich palette and whose voice deserves to be heard by a wider audience.
One of Wales' finest bards of the moment."

Paul Steffan Jones, author of *Lull of the Bull, The Trigger-Happiness* and *Otherlander*.

"You are so sparse. You leave so much to us and never waste a word. Your descriptions are so visually rich and vibrant ... So full of colour and texture....
You have become a master painter."

Jo Davies, author of *To Forget With Grace.*

*

"Richard's poetry simply hums with the appreciation of place, of nature, wildlife and the ways in which we humans slip into the landscape.
The poems are beautiful. Elegiac, sometimes sparsely constructed, evocative and thoughtful, these are poems that have the capacity to take you out of your world and into that of the poet."

Marc Mordey, author of *Marcism Today*

*

"Richard's poems reach out to you. He manages to gift the reader with carefully crafted word portraits, 'eavesdropped from another world'. One day, I should love to hear him read these poems in the summer setting of a peaceful wood with stream nearby.
Exquisite work."

Anne Marie Butler, working poet and landscape artist, winner of the 2017 R.S.Thomas Poetry Prize.

"Richard Wheeler's poems are keen-eyed, arresting, linguistically adroit, and utterly distinctive in their way of juxtaposing image and idea. They explore themes of place, time, memory, desire, and – in many cases – the role of poetry and visual art in creating a jump-cut mental scenography where these are strangely intermixed.
An impressive collection and one that offers striking thoughts and perceptions on every page."

Chris Norris. Emeritus Professor of Philosophy, Cardiff University.

DEDICATION & ACKNOWLEDGMENTS

For her deep involvement with my writing and criticism and advice on this manuscript I am especially grateful to Jo Davies. I'm also immensely grateful to the extraordinary artist, Jane Corsellis, for kindly agreeing to the use of 'Walker on the Shore, Pembrokeshire' on the cover of this collection. I'd also like to thank Anne Marie Butler, Paul Steffan Jones, Kathy Miles and Chris Norris for their generous words and on-going encouragement. Marc Mordey for the same, and for introducing me to Cambria Books. Too, Ruth Sharpe for her eagle-eyed proofreading of the entire text. The importance of a safe, supportive, public forum for a poet to trial his/her work can't be overstated and I'm hugely grateful to the co-organisers of the Cellar Bards spoken word event - Dave Urwin and Jackie Biggs - for working so hard to keep this alive. Poetry needs to be heard!

Further back still, the poetry masterclass run by Gillian Clarke and Carol Ann Duffy got me on my way; a hand written response from The Rialto put wind in my sails; as did *Anouar Brahem is Mowing* securing a berth in the Brian Dempsey Memorial Competition Anthology 2021 - *Horses of a different colour*. Beyond that I'm every bit as grateful to all those others (friends, fellow poets) who have shown their belief and interest in these poems and whose response has led to a change in my circuitry: to press the publishing button!

where each flick of a switch

is a separation

I of Modern Nature

THE POEMS

Affirmation

First time in a while, this need to write.

In a sprawling thoroughfare of urban parkland
my unobtrusive lens spills images of human need
directly onto the printed page.

"Be a witness to my life"
is screamed or cowed a thousand times.

Later, in a darkroom of my own
this hitherto dormant pencil once again sees light,
'validate me, validate me';
disparate needs distilled to this.

Bedsit

Hazard a guess in the stillness
the after-quiet,

watch the nonchalance of pike
grip the shadows

archaic prisoners of the reeds;

in such depths, these nightjar hours
a pact to break this torpor,

slip these shackles,
steal upstream
above the river's morbid confluence,

to sunlit shallows, shoals

of turbo-d flicker-fish
deft and free,

a tentative dipping of the toe
the aftermath,

one rung at a time
and not what might have been.

Anouar Brahem is Mowing

This see-through lounge
holds all the clues,

with shrubberies to circle
in one window,
chicane of statues in the next;

across the room's bellied ouds
beyond this depth of field
Baluch rugs, piano, music stand

Anouar mows metronomically,

and what of the margins
around the pool
left frayed, unkempt,
dissonant.

Hearsay has it
that if you leave La Gare
ear to the ground,
climbing these forlorn streets
peeling an orange as you walk,

by its nakedness
a grace of dialects will greet you,

time signatures
eavesdropped
from another world
through breezy sash windows.

Sea Glass

The estuary has gorged,
a somnambulant millpond
holding its watery breath,
replete, framed, widescreen.

We drape ourselves,
Pooh sticks height, midstream
mesmerized by this age old
ritual, six pairs of eyes
fully present in the past
alive in the swirling current,
flowing across and behind
quiet minds, clocking the renewal,
with a sense that the world creates itself
from moment to moment,

eddies conniving to outflank,
pull rank, settle once and for all
their brackish exchanges.
All the while this clockwork rhythm
effortlessly frames our days,
fleeting lives, waiting and watching
for the compass to turn,
ocean to take back what it's owed,
and then some.

Hikers pass us on the bridge
dust enamelled boots, caked
grass seed crowded eyelets
their owners weary, chatty, enlivened,
eyes only for this juicy place,
a shared love of the shore
the beating pulse,
sea glass polished, scrutinized
held safe.

Biophilia

If I hold a mirror up
to a spider's soul, busy

in her handed-down-ness,
unconscious guile, illiterate

of whether home or trap,

do her intentions
become clear.

Or to this virtual moth
camouflaged as bark

stripe for stripe,
does it recognise itself,

boundaries of form,
fullness of the deceit,

feel free to live
without fear.

Or to this fistful of fluff
buffeted across oceans,

unseduced by landforms,
in the eye of storms and lead,

on course for these eaves,

the same ones
as last year,

would it repeat the feat,
the journey
if it knew of life's death.

And turning the glass
will I pause to draw breath,
disavow hubris and reason,
evolution's smoke
and mirrors.

The kingfisher knows nothing
while you're passing
of its allure, or the tides
per se

And for my next Trick

The visionary almost fell apart at the last
undone by a sense of fate, a bounce,
crossing palms, a wager, hear this
to control an entity
programmed to within an inch of its life,
an audacious heist, a slingshot
slung past this besmirched earth
not once but twice,
tracking far-off dust tails,
long gone contrails
on the coat tails of a pre-selected
stridulating comet,
in its binary wake
inordinate brains with cracked heels,
furrowed brows, orchestra soloists,
microbiologists daring to believe
daren't even breathe, questions
questions, all for life's answers
and the kudos of kudos,
clocking the arc of a park swing,
left arm spin, path of a mortarboard
where are we, Si?
Heart in mouth, a foot wrong
please God
their baby thrumming in the blackness
on a dependable axis,
fuelled by solar panels and what we know
of gravitational pull (and much else besides)
playing seven year catch-up, then
hypnotised into a light sleep spin
in deep space hibernation,

on the surface as self-contained
as a swift on the wing,
zeroing in through the silent cacophony
no fuel stops, running repairs
airport lounges, whims or prayers,
now coming in to land, if you will
upon a layer of sintered ice-dust
a postage stamp of unknown mass
itself travelling through time at 50,000 kmh.

What could possibly go wrong?

Abermawr

Come, lower your ear
to this skin of stones
and what lies beneath,

but first, dance with me
on the bruised, moist sand,
makeshift stage
between submerged forest,
salt preserved, reticent
(yet perfect for petanque),
and the shoreline's
buried treasure,
unspoken for.

Incoming tide will soon enough
erase all traces of our tryst,
drowned footsteps
pointing to the berm of pebbles
warmed by a glancing sun,
where butterflies cavort and sip
the trickle of spring water
a wingspan beneath them.

Here, lie on your side
and lower your ear
to the dry stones
protecting the chatter of cooling life,
and when you're done
transform your cupped hand
into an ice cream scoop,
to best unearth the hidden gems.

Clearing the Traps

Sprung metal,
sugar rush of fish skins
resurge of a feral world,
animal ley lines, surely.
Meanwhile, I of modern nature,
stripped of bearings,
known givens.

Headlong, snapped the necks,
blood on the ash tracks
mill grain long in the memory,
trapped hither and thither
here taken out, kith and kin
save for a fur-bled, bead head
ship's figurehead and tail,
spent trap an empty carriage.

Others sclerotic, poison-dazed
and I, in the moment, so overrun
the mind now crazed, irrational
dreams of empty reservoirs, famine,
of no clock to turn back,
no clutch of eggs,
chapter and verse,
a kind of biblical hell.

Pale Blue Dot

You find me
perhaps where I found myself,
thumb out on the dusk freeway
way back when,
living between the creased folds
of a worn Eastern Seaboard map,
New Hampshire, Virginia, Florida
the worm of felt tip progress
born of irrational optimism,
dearth of life lived;
Union Jack-draped backpack,
Dark Side of the Moon t-shirt,
sparse pubic beard,
chewing the fat in trucks, rest areas
over music, scale, man's place.
What I would have given
for Voyager 1's pale blue dot
still a decade or more in the making,
for its unarguable perspective
within a ray of light,
the luck of a sunbeam.

House Sitting

Scald of water
the hand's raw, bruised bloom
as startling as the early blossom,
like flying a hawk to the fist, gloveless,
or the view over the rolling collar of sea,
you can pick the moment
that opens to this other world,

signatures of strangers
scrawled, without explanatory notes,
on deep vermillion walls
porous to the vixen's otherworldly screams,
slubs in heavy curtains
silence of heavy doors
air pocket punctured, held fire-tight
the sucker punch
as rooms give up their secrets
in a slow release,
framed back stories
woven in wheel-thrown porcelain,
slipcast Japanese vases,
rugs from Ladakh
spare line drawings, breaths on eggshell,

and on the conservatory's lee wall,
moonbeam raking the headland grass,
the same sea view, in bygone sepia daylight
rustic lean-to cabin, open to the elements

gap toothed man replete on wicker chair
alive to where the sun alights
on a wall, and when,
present in this landscape.

Analogue Poetry

Christmas Eve
and, craving aloneness
I imbibe analogue poetry.

Words, symbiotic with the page,
Heaney, Oswald, Sheers
tumble over the fireside sofa
a portable quiet
smuggled in to these alien surroundings
like so many Trojan horses.

Little has atrophied
in this monetised hunting lodge,
Tatlers, baronial art,
brooding mountains
looming through high windows,
tapestry foot followers of the hunt,
mahogany walls with trophy heads,
Diana in virginal cobalt blue.
A language as real to the clientele
as these travelling companions are to me.

Home

Whose life prints are these
hanging in the air
in long term spaces,
ingrained in deep walls
adept at holding in the warmth
less so the past,

whose foot prints trod
this goat-narrow winding staircase
past bruised wattle and daub,
and with what urgency,
eight treads of hope
across the generations
(Baker's dozen
in the microfiche archive)

who sought out the neighbours voices
housed in the shared inglenook
found solace in their misery,
or, breaking off from work
to heed the blackbird's feats
cascading down chimney's artery,

what of the family of five
custodians of this cherished space
beneath thatch and screeching swifts,
farrier, seamstress, layman, midwife
lives cut from the same salmon brick

shared stories, hand-me-downs
graveyard,

whose was the abandoned shoe
unyielding, curled, discarded
in the loft - and why?

Pre-dawn, military rumbles by
on Salisbury-bound manoeuvres
rattling Sugar soap bottles
and others in their sights,
whilst the present occupant
sleeps with the hitherto dead space
occupied not by people,
but CDs, bookshelves, KEF speakers,
art on fragile soap-soft walls.

Ty Canol Wood

Buried deep in our psyche
yet not *so* deep,
the primordial woodland
disarms us with its voice,
silencing ours with connections
near lost.

Beneath oak, lichen canopy,
foraging and fossicking as we go
in achingly gentle stillness,
hands plunge, finger-deep
into cool moss pools,
heron-necked stumps soar
picked clean in death,
sculptures in search of light.

Lone oak time-capsule,
carapaced hourglass
for now inactive,
camouflaged
in the shadow of slumbering granite,
umbilical thread intact,
permanence in situ.

Dormant chrysalis,
what will become of you?

Today I choose

not to engage with you,
not to share your wonder with my child,
roll your shell around my palm.
On another day, mood, season
I search for you,
a needle. Nothing.

Picasso's 'Dove of Peace'

(finding peace in a Burns ward)

The light filament, though dimmed
excretes a white heat glare,
worse, it corrupts

the room becomes known,

fragments of ideas
jostle and die,

darkness, when it arrives
allows in light, the mind
sifts – rakes over, cools

is free to wander.

A lithograph of Picasso's *Colombe Volant*
floats out of the murk,
containing nothing
but sparse, airy, carefree lines,
hope stretched in a blue crayon,

an olive branch grasped,
imperceptibly.

A moth at the window
tethered to the newly white filament,
spoon-fed,

within, a surgeon hovers,
overseeing the wrapping of indignant,
weeping, would-be skin,

a single eyelid
tears up corners of a brittle mind.

Look me in the eye if you will,
beyond what you see
a now unfamiliar face,
hear me – still.

I of Modern Nature

I of modern nature
fashioning a life
within the margins,

torn between
the unsewn seams
of primal and frivolous,

rusty in both
if truth be told,
layers of disconnect

a film of surface,

where each flick of a switch
is a separation,

a kind of no-mans-land
of convenience,
seed bed for hubris

the go-it-alone species,
taxonomy now a mystery,

a tourist's pick 'n mix
of trade-offs and pixels
the new cradle to grave,

ashes to ashes
the old currency.

A Walk at Dusk

How quickly
the night sky descends

light incrementally reduced,
orphaned, overrun.

Hemmed into rural lanes,
leaning in, to your brother's
shouldered darkness

unknowable weight,
pulse-slowing hell,

we vie with bats for a spare signal
to a chaotic far-off ward,
suspended selves, neon lights
gatekeepers lost to protocol.
First names, case files
are all that remain.

And somehow it's not enough
To settle for this stasis,
but instead to slice a perfect cube
of blackness out of the night
supplanting it with one of white.

The Colours of a Meal

Spatchcock pigeon,
breastbone
emptied of flesh,
unedifying
dustbowl of feathers
separated in death,
quilt, quill, a foot,
encumbrances
to the torn, warm
rose pulp-roe,

bibless, bristling hawk
has fed, fled
life's onward march,
clock watching
maggots
pustular buttermilk ghosts
riding the rip and shizzle
capricious luck;
nest lining birds
greedy for life
ask no questions,
and the nearby
whiffling geese
content to graze
provide no send-off, just
a smoky mackerel backdrop
to this vicissitude.

Alumni

I shall go to my death
pulling goose-grass
beneath Cornus *kousa chinensis.*
Privileged, waist high
in work that can wait,
the wrapped, bract canopy
guardian angel, confidant,
a life choice and more away
from land the colour of military,
world dressed in geometry
of managing the unknown.
Disembarking, unfazed
platoon wreathed
in careworn smiles, now
arms dropped, pen raised
covenant-signing photo shoot,
and that inclusive, opt-in smile
from way, way back.

On the edge of Hope
(i.m. Barbara Slade)

Along a fly-tipped rat run,
despoiled rural outreach of suburbia,
a woman in a child's frame
propels a pedal-less child's bicycle
with a rhythmic sweep of her legs,
marshalling this lane of her childhood
with a protective ghillie's eye,
twitchy, outcross hound.

Beguiling misanthrope,
proud vigilante throwback
able to zero a rifle, tie a fly,
dress a pheasant, stand her ground
and when she has cause to buy
"With as much fat as you can muster!"
Unyielding then, and now
staring out from all our pasts,
her photographic memory
and eye (not too far-fetched to muse)
with all the attributes of a spy.

Held up by her deaf, indomitable back
fuelled hooligans track her heels,
in loud, bravado, witless wheels,
no way past now, until at road's bend
the bridge of her youth, where the lure
of pitching guile and invested fly

to kiss these languid waters,
trick an *out thought* trout, now meets with
leery, sweary mouths
the who, how, where of saved lives
in a real war zone
not worth a hill of beans.

Boulevard

The florist in me
pines for the medium of clay,
a vase in each room
for the eyes to rest
to hold back time;

perhaps it's the boulevard,
busy floral windows
where bouquets of immediacy
exit like so many clouds
of butterflies, ushered out
in fragrant whorls,

liminal, for now
the telling of story,
symbiosis, not of scooped clay
a cornflower's elegance,
but the oxygen of *to and from.*
Wait a while, and they may stand
sublime and proud,
moments of collected grace
for the mind to stretch out,
a vase in the here and now.

Take Me Out, Why Don't You

Summer night
and there's dread in the eyes
of feral headlights
carving their burning name
through the tamed landscape,

this length of twisted metal road,
failing to contain
a lunging double bullet
unmanned, bearing down
through the drug addled fog,

my smudged electrics
an unwanted lighthouse steer,
twin beam tugging at recognition,
a fragile foothold in this world,
dry in the mouth, drugged foot flat
engine bursting, lights
seared
into a slow
film
shutter
speed

too much time,
out of time,
not before time

we meet, at a bend
across my car's bows
this crossroads of life

another decision
a different outcome.

Colonies

Treading the high coast path
above Marros beach
through sloe-bush groves,
the clean wake-up of citrus tangerine Crocosmias,
warm punch of sun-filled bracken.
Funnel spider fortresses, their silk cloud breaths
spun deep into latticed coconut gorse,
an abandoned, still slavered stick
kisses, interrogates loose termite sand
calls to arms translucent orange defenders.
On hand, and on speaking terms
two sibling benches meet each other's gaze,
dependent on a keen ear or minds-eye
for a different world view.
At arm's reach, plump tart blackberries
stupid on the tongue, their juices linger
all the way down the heady privet staircase.
Fresh sieved release of shingle,
bubbling curlews, oystercatcher's squeals
crumbling and colluding
and the crustacean's dual life
for now undislodgeable on slabs of millennia.

Yards to the east, aged nudists
meerkats in their rocky enclave
one, baboon shaped, all rump, high chest
mincing beefsteak bravado.

Fair Game

In as much as you may recognise
the angle of the wind,
attention of the sun

outside the corm-womb
that these things are sewn into,
the curate's egg that is life,

such a certain seventh sense
will only count for so much.

Following the ignition
of burst-open life,
there is no un-breaking of the soil
no retracting of the snout-shoot
from the blistered bark
or the membrane of memory,
you are fair game.

milvus milvus

A solitary red kite
holds the wind,
ethereal puppeteer,
poised sugar whisperer
scouring, scouring
this patchwork of sourdough fells,
ochre-earth, burnt bracken-red.

Swiss army wind sails
tooth the cinnamon horizon,

panoply of farms and farmsteads,
pin pricks of sedentary wool,
gnarled hawthorn silhouettes,
raindrops on barbed wire,

clouds draw the colours' blind,
Preseli basin a ping-pong interior.

Balletic to the core,
the kite drifts, glides and falls,
molten caramel in a blustery vortex,
controlled vision,
drops on a dime,
unerringly.

Vows

The wrong name spills
from a priest's lips,
the heavy-lifting of vows

left for another day,
for a couple with these same
God-given names, whose time.

But this is now, late Fall
a Catholic seminary in Pennsylvania,
early snow, sacred chant
backdrop to a pre-nuptial blessing, of sorts.

And fresh from Confessional
the bombshell, like an adoption mix-up,
bleeds into the loved-up room,
and a couple falls at the first.

Outside these managed walls,
beyond austere, manicured lawns,
Jack & Diane pulses
across America,
calling to prayer

lovers, eager for their chance,
in a bar in Pittsburgh, steel city
the wrong name took his
to the Devil's riff,

sowing a seed of doubt
an earworm, cuckoo's egg.

Overwintering

Huddle of life on the hills,
livestock serenaded
in breaths of cloud condensate,
circular breathing
winter closing down

closing in,

those with a price
ushered off these wanton slopes
to a woodchip corral
and temporary survival

Spade slicing caked soil,
circling weather-broken
salvias, penstemons, cannas

carcasses
of their former pastel selves,
root ball lifted intact
in time, into sand
hustled away

life bulb preserved
turned off

Bone-dry garage,
a woollen flying jacket
sees off another season

unscarred,

and a clock-smith's hands
make light work
of the scrambler's electrics

disengaged over winter;
the whole, dust sheet wrapped,
visited by darkness and mice.

Relationship with a Chicken

The cutlery
understands intimately
what to expect,
knows its way round
separating tibia and femur
flesh from the former;
knife through menisci,
assorted ligaments, tendons,
at one with the task
slides behind the fibula
once, a million times;
this cut
for that cartilage
with that texture
fleshiness, chew ability,
a known return
inside and out
back of my hand.

Mushrooming

An autumn quartering
of a meadow
familiar to me

inadvertently
laying down a scent trail
better read than I,

my path in the making

criss-crosses
pin tracks
of a ticking fox

moving through. Lawless.

Harebell, field scabious,
crested dog's tail, selfheal;

in the quiet sward,
meadow's leeward flank,

steadfast trundle
of a nocturnal goods train
single gauge, slalom
underbelly groove

unmistakeably
a badger's world,
each indifferent
to the unctuous

alabaster snow caps
I stoop to predate.

And when I draw level,
blade-hand poised
above the spores,

moist talc drawn
toward the thumb
adhering to the fingers,

decades fall away at a stroke.

As kids we would trek
the joined-up, still dark fields
elm stile marking the way
to the one that counted;

lodged in the brain's tongue
chocolate coral gills
upturned and turned
in fat and brine
umami on the lips,

far from mealy mouthed
feral smell of broken iron

burnt and of the earth,
the tang and salt sizzle
of deliverance.

Language that Unlocks
(in the company of John Adams, composer)

I found myself seeking out his ears
as if the secret lay within,
the configuration, perhaps, a clue,
an alternative window to the soul
filtering the sureness of seeing
of hearing a feeling
patois of being,
of how life is played back
the chosen language always
that of sound,
of syncopation,
circuitry fully formed,
a voice fully heard,
of language that unlocks
unravels its meaning
through menace and turmoil
stylus' pickup,
a keening.

Letter from Somewhere

Forgive me this once
if I come across as monosyllabic.

From this chair you know so well
you catch me peering out
at the queueing planes,
afar yet complicit.

The dog below is hurling insults,
irrespective of who will listen

caught in the crossfire
of smog and injustice,
nineteen storeys down,

evolution playing catchup,
brought to life in the thumbwheel
crosshairs of my binoculars.

Now bickering with other feral dogs
sniffing on plastic turf

duped by what?
exactly.

You never see their eyes,
these dogs; the head
dropped like a lowered crane
nose attentive
to the impoverished soil,
the nowhere soil.

Averting our gaze,
pariahs, to be tolerated.

Time was when
I admired their fight, insolence
deferring perhaps
to a proud demeanour,
my shame of human consequence,

that it is their world too.

You'll recall
the camels feeding on these walls,
yet to feel fed I crave other people's nature,
bullfinch, snow leopard, dolphins
sit on my screen
for those dog days
when thunder fills the air,

my tastes logged consciously;

yet time passes,
habits shape truth
balance becomes jettisoned,
replaced by a new truth.

Glassy-eyed, incurious
a conductor without a baton,
I watch the tentacled traffic
light up the arteries.
At midday.

And as I write, the smog's veil is lifting,
more planes will surely gather,
and the memorized urban ocean,
uninterrupted to the horizon
seemingly preserved in aspic,
will release its own secrets

the dark arts, of tenements
flattened for others,
planners filling boots and gaps,
a whim in a sea of whims,
the cubist canvas of grey and glass
jigsaw of what is in, what is out,
a puff of dust
my whole perspective.

Which is why today,
I can only offer you false roses.

Turning Over

I live by the sea
in a place where there's sun,
turning over
in each dawn's
slow striptease
the tenor of the day,
an Arabic lute
easing down
thinking and feeling,
heavy lidded acquiescence,
slow cooker horizon,
burgundy luggers hard wired
the day long.
Oatmeal, cobalt,
steady breath
through a dandelion's skirts
seeds of stars,

bruised vermillion
held in a skylight,
Dvorak, Janacek, Mahler.
Nightfall. Wet room washes away
the nothingness of the day,
bourbon (dixie cup),
whitewashed ceiling.

At what point did she step away from life.

Unbidden

I'm offered an improbably tiny hand
new to this world,

closed, unknowing.

I hold it like so, preciously
between thumb and forefinger,

can it be this nascent dextrous corm,
these still furled fronds
for now shut tight, blind
shy, may one day
climb a kite into the sky,
hold a lover's face
touch another's heart,
squeeze
a
trigger.
Guide a Palomino,
gesture
supplication,
tapered pianist's fingers
adhered in hope,
hope unspoken,
this un-woken bud
one half of an antiphonal choir
channelling love and angst,
hamstrung, hands wrung

at the beck and call
of needs and stuff
unbidden.

All things arrive here
resolve here,

life manifested
in a fist, or
inclusively open
like a butterfly
kiss.

Last stop on the line,
one more time to worry a button,
run hands through a mannerism,
take out the garbage,
link frail fingers,
savour the touch of linen
clenched or flat palmed,
and should you be so lucky
to say, place your hand
in mine, please.

The Grounding Line

Beneath this single sky
is it any wonder,
across the millennia
there is a conversation going on.

[The point at which glaciers and ice shelves start to float is
the Grounding Line. The location of the grounding line is
important, because mass loss from Antarctica is strongly linked to
changes in the ice shelves and their grounding lines. Change in the
grounding line can result in very rapid changes in glacier and ice-
shelf behaviour.]

An Omen

In a year when the gooseberries
were unresolved,
the relied upon flesh
instead held as unspent bullets,
we slept back to back
the smalls of our spines
obdurate hulls in the night,
firepit of silence,

in these moments
did your eyes close to the owl's cry
or stare at the unseen tree,
imagining soundless flight
before crossing into sleep.

In the fetid roof space
pipistrelles pitched tight to the joists,
a trug lies beached, upturned,
once the epicentre of our lives
its worm-trailed willow
etched with the sugary ink
of bruised souls, pressed into service,
strawberries culled early from straw beds
marble rose-white above the red earth
now teased from the calyx
undressed in the kitchen's shadows,
toying and vying, seeping with intent
love is when you relent, you said.

Never far from the conversation
the willow's spoils spilling into foothills
over the hewn oak table,
diced with care into the pan's alchemy
buttery smoke, garlic, ceps, cumin,
creating something to believe in,
barometer of where we were
fastening our fate to the season.

And then the conversation ran out,
fruit went unpicked
trug untroubled.

Later in the year
on a morning filled with cross currents,
you placed the medlar fruit on trays to blet,
the next day you had gone.

Second Skin

In my field of vision
a youth reflects
off the darkened carriage window,
a convenient second skin
through which I find myself
vicariously drawn in.
Curled into a device
no part of him disowns,
even when the prairie's light returns,
smudged shapes finding their truth
in a milky dishcloth dawn,
this shifting palimpsest
into which we're born
holds no allure.

Foreboding

You hear it first
in the spinning jenny,
the gathering of the fabric,
an easy relationship of spindles and wheel
weaving their resolute magic,
spools spilling time
from light
to dark o'clock,
circadian rhythms intact.

Until that is, the yarn price fell,
unspun thread, a cat's cradle
torn from its moorings,
railed against
under oath and hammer blows,
last vestiges, last rites.
And they would turn in their graves
to know that, downstream
past the rivers of windmills,
factory gates and graphene,
a committee of vultures
hangs on our every noiseless word,
humans reduced to bystanders
drained of colour,
no longer in the loop,
sleepwalking.

The Stonemason

Eye to hand, hand to eye
improvising, no sheet music
the weft of stone observed
properties logged,
tapped, clocked intuitively,
sifting, weighing
for shape and fit, not if but when,
a re-working, recycling;
here an otter in repose,
sinuous flank, opening and closing, ponderous
wall of ante-sculpture,
animal essence, primal man
at one with the land, eye to hand,
full trust in both. Just is.

The Potter
(for J.G)

Just beyond the 5-bar gate
world weariness is put on hold
barred entry to a courtyard garden
vibrant with heady collisions; wood stacked
for the down-draught kiln,
traditional terracotta, kaolin, salvias, tribal art.
One man's love affair with shape and truth
all inhaled gratefully. Instantly.

Thinking of this a week later,
sinuous paths lined with ideas
acidanthera running riot,
glazed pots fecund with succulents,
I toast an eye that sees nature,
ideas, art as one; hears Bach's cello Concerto No.1
at a west African market; embraces three generations
garrulous, around a Mediterranean table,
here feasting on cold, hot colours.

Chairs

There's nothing the day chair
reveals of the past,
but in the stippled fabric,
the armrest nap,
memories rub at the surface,
thread of plum roses, bare now
and life before these walls
is left unsaid,
though not of what,
gives way
to the urgency of the now,
the TV's friendly fire
hurries on, the fading of the day

A tungsten afternoon

beyond the creaking bay window
a blistering sun wreaks havoc,
mind emptying, indiscriminate,
muffled flight trail
the only show in town.

On the handkerchief lawn
charcoaled gorse sticks,
bounty from the fells burn-off,
spread-eagled art
threatening to reignite.

Within the apple tree's drifting shade
a throw-draped rocking chair
has been home these eleven days,
my body at one with its lines,
stretched, crumpled
held inside soft contours,
books, pencils, shawls for company

Commissioned
six weeks to the day
from handshake to the call,
she stood (for it was *she*)
high backed, multi-stemmed
occupying just these pencil lines

burnt honeyed oak
flecks of darker grain running
proud, like split rice
up a Welsh stick spine,
soft elm seat, saddle steak

the whole, poised elegance
worth a thousand photos,
backlit
on a turning pedestal

55

The chair that takes my weight
is an itinerant,
a blow-in
schlepping from pillar to post.

For a week this school hand-me-down,
this adoptee, is ours.

Upcycled, glossy narrowboat green,
cream embroidered slats,
mauve flowers (stamens of whimsy),

two accompanying diaries
in satchels slung down the back,
even street numbers record adoptive words
odd, photos and sketches.
Up in the garret,
images to hand,
I write poems on the easel
to give the odds a voice.

My six year old: "Must everything be
explained?"

Save for revelations from a C19th dictionary
a *blunt clown, fillet of silk, idle prate, tuz,*
which I set down *in short hints,*
week thirty six is left empty.

The elderly lady
sits in a director's chair
her back to me
staring at the sea,

on Sundays I used to
tend her grave,
just as I did her
pre-deceased daughter.

September's monotone sea
ensures her thoughts aren't broken,
a grey seal may shape them,
momentarily.

These days I often revisit
the spot by the sea,
less so her grave
though that may change.

Splayed-orb Assassin

The canny, splayed-orb assassin is stationed,
a cerebral waterboatman awash a delicate land-locked grid.
Suspended surreally in the ether, this menacing tactician
(a free spinning, pin-head sac of guile)
punches way above her featherlight weight.
Monster, mathematician and thread artist
she spins and lures, outwits and conjures
everything from nothing.
At her behest trigger-happy sensors
flex and slack, tauten and track
then, on tightening the noose,
she avariciously straw-sucks the warm innards
from those too cussed and curious for their own good,
blown off course to end up as trussed detritus.

Rain-filled skies have unpacked and moved on,
in their wake death holds sway within the frenzied run-off.
Sheltering under a leaf, the perfectionist hangs, linked
to the business end by a hair's breadth thread
gauging all-comers. Beads inter-lock,
meld the nodes of her silken fetish parlour.
The bloated whole sags and tests, shapes
to bend and flex - it's all or nothing.
Husks of decay perch forlornly
like abandoned prayer flags.
Later, re-entering the fray
in a blur of cross stitch and innate maths,
she assiduously shores up the lines of offence,
making good this cowardly chess board.

Machynlleth (Artists Valley)

A stone's throw
from these bearded chimney stacks,
jackdaws grey, graceless,
scuttle and lurch,
tilted beaks eking slim pickings
between paving slabs;

vecchi, in all but name,
here, their prospects intertwined
with the winter streets.

No more than an osprey flight
from nearby Ynys-hir, inland
Tolkien hinterland,
contoured woodland,
swatch of moss sponge
awash with life on the move;

and always
this stillness of sound.

Seven miles, as the crow flies
past the town's landmark timepiece,
lives hitched to its heartbeat,
time immemorial

human time - bookends -
ricocheting, embedding,
registering life on the quarter.

Duty of care,
hourglass of bottled fury,
pavements graced by memory.

Burning the Library of Life

September's song
above the woodland's stolen leaves,
honey-fluted jester holds court
calling into being these trees,
in broken and unbroken lines
sure-footed cadences,
closing out all-comers,

liquid tones clean and true
flooding, melding
the culled, cold post-wildfire,
and into the gaps an epitaph
declared from a different tree,
before and after photograph.

I am a nemophilist
alive to the spores, scrapings, tell-tale signs
skyline's perennial moving graph,
light-shaped cameos, snuffed-out exits
in thrall to how this or that (unit of life)
summons the wherewithal.

Whisper it to the turtles,
polar bears, bush crickets, dormice
but here amongst the dis-eased ash
lies a different path
that has no truck with
burning the library of life.

Spring. A songbird sings
unscarred by dreams,
stopping me in my tracks,
insouciance, counter threnody
bass symphony,
pitch perfect in the key of life,
dancing in defiance
above the woodland floor,
the sum, equilibrium of sorts
for each death - a life and more.

[A more philosophical way of viewing biodiversity is that it
represents the knowledge learned by evolving species over
millions of years about how to survive through the vastly varying
environmental conditions Earth has experienced. Seen like that,
experts warn, humanity is currently "burning the library of life."
The Guardian.]

Anatomy of Wood

Wild roses grew there

briars and pale pink *Rugosa*
circling a makeshift lean-to woodshed.

Upon the bovine chain saw cutting out,
hear the sharp, dull *thwack*
in the axe's degrading of each log,
the woodsman using its weight,
and weight alone,
to seer diagonal cuts on the clockface
reading the grain, lines of release and flow
points of attachment.

Steel cone is placed at the ash's heart,
with a single blow
fruit segments fall away obligingly,

the method is what delights:
tools, rationale, science.

Yet in the hollowed sockets
synovial joints and tearings
his son glimpses a Zen charcoal bowl,
sanded anniversaries like watermarks,
woodturner's lathe creating alchemy,
an opening up of worlds
morphing science and art,
of cherry hardwood chessmen

the words of Apsley Cherry-Garrard and Saki
but above all, the minimalist charcoal bowl
elevated kestrel wings on a pinhead base,
paper, paper thin.

Arboretum

field notes in mid winter

Trees certain of their space
gold sunlight a tall trees prize,

cartoons spread-eagled,
child friendly, grotesque

beeches with painterly skirts
a dhow's masts, sails lowered,
dropped. Anchored.
Plants drowned in winter shade

hornbeam's coffee-chrysalis husks,
crisp curled sheaths,
pupated buds mislaid
magicked along the bough,

marble kidney balustrade,
bone-cold to the touch,
peel and curl of paperbark.

Birds scratching, rootling
nearby thrum-drumming
woodpecker,

blackbird fastidious
swiping clean the worm
metronomically,

ravens making merry,
one with Goya-like menace
on nearby acer,

robin in purple pittosporum,
finches busy in thickets
in the game,

child-high gingko,
fallen leaves neat like municipal
cubicle-discarded smalls.

Arboreal cathedrals,
our sedge crane necks
ratcheted higher than the dilating eye,

winter honeysuckle,
bamboo for dens
"Coming, ready or not"

toffee fungi spores,
sodden, molten, putrid.

Tree skins

fissured, spiralled,
tear-dropped,
pocked,
riven,
gargoyled,
snake-barked

elephant hide.

Listen to Richard reading a selection
of these poems at the link below:

www.soundcloud.com/iofmodernnature

Richard can be contacted by email at:
ascertain1@gmail.com

Lightning Source UK Ltd.
Milton Keynes UK
UKHW021547030222
398152UK00005B/132